Caring for My Pet

Hamster

Jill Foran

and Katie Gillespie

MEDIA ENHANCED BOOKS
AV2 BY WEIGL
ADDED VALUE • AUDIO VISUAL

www.av2books.com

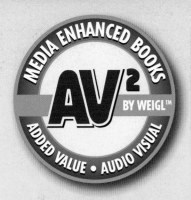

MEDIA ENHANCED BOOKS
AV²
BY WEIGL™
ADDED VALUE • AUDIO VISUAL

Go to **www.av2books.com**, and enter this book's unique code.

BOOK CODE

D 5 6 9 0 0 0

AV² by Weigl brings you media enhanced books that support active learning.

AV² provides enriched content that supplements and complements this book. Weigl's AV² books strive to create inspired learning and engage young minds in a total learning experience.

Your AV² Media Enhanced books come alive with...

Audio
Listen to sections of the book read aloud.

Video
Watch informative video clips.

Embedded Weblinks
Gain additional information for research.

Try This!
Complete activities and hands-on experiments.

Key Words
Study vocabulary, and complete a matching word activity.

Quizzes
Test your knowledge.

Slide Show
View images and captions, and prepare a presentation.

... and much, much more!

Published by AV² by Weigl
350 5th Avenue, 59th Floor
New York, NY 10118
Website: www.av2books.com www.weigl.com

Library of Congress Control Number: 2013953119
ISBN 978-1-4896-0616-7 (hardcover)
ISBN 978-1-4896-0617-4 (softcover)
ISBN 978-1-4896-0618-1 (single user eBook)
ISBN 978-1-4896-0619-8 (multi-user eBook)

Printed in the United States of America in North Mankato, Minnesota
1 2 3 4 5 6 7 8 9 0 18 17 16 15 14

012014
WEP301113

Project Coordinator: Katie Gillespie
Design and Layout: Mandy Christiansen

Every reasonable effort has been made to trace ownership and to obtain permission to reprint copyright material. The publishers would be pleased to have any errors or omissions brought to their attention so that they may be corrected in subsequent printings.

Weigl acknowledges Getty Images as its primary image supplier for this title.

Caring for My Pet

Hamster

Contents

Hamsters and Happiness

Hamsters are small, soft, and adorable. They are the most popular small pets in the world. Not only are they cuddly and cute, hamsters are also relatively simple to care for. Because they are clean and inexpensive, they are a good choice for a first time pet owner.

Although they are entertaining pets, hamsters are also a big responsibility. It takes commitment and caring to own any pet. Once you have a hamster, you must be willing to look after her for the rest of her life. This includes feeding, playing with, grooming, and caring for her. If you are able to take the time, owning a hamster can be fun and rewarding.

There are more than **20 types** of hamster living in nature.

Only **five breeds** of hamster are commonly kept as pets.

A hamster's life span is about **two to four years.**

Syrian hamsters are **4 to 7 inches** long. (10 to 18 centimeters)

It was not until **1995** that Djungarian hamsters were widely sold as pets.

Some hamster breeds, such as the Campbell's Russian hamster, can live in pairs or groups.

Hamster History

Hamsters belong to a large group of animals called **rodents**. Some breeds of hamsters have been around for hundreds of years. The first ever found by humans was a Syrian hamster. It was discovered in the deserts of Syria, near a place called Aleppo. In Syria, there are many wild hamsters living under the surface of the sand.

In nature, golden hamsters have underground burrows.

In 1839, a **zoologist** named George Robert Waterhouse presented the London Zoological Society with a female golden hamster. She was also found near Aleppo. However, no one else could find evidence of the wild Syrian hamsters. Many people thought they had become **extinct**.

Nearly 100 years later, a mother Syrian hamster and her 11 babies were found and captured by Dr. Israel Aharoni. These hamsters had been **burrowed** far below the Syrian desert, near Aleppo. Doctor Aharoni was able to keep three of these hamsters. Within a short period, they had produced hundreds of baby hamsters.

The **first recorded** Syrian hamster discovery occurred in the **late 1700s**.

The **first hamsters** were brought to the U.S. in **1938**.

Hamsters have been domesticated for **more than 70 years**.

Squirrels, beavers, prairie dogs, and mice are all members of the rodent group. It is the most varied of all the mammal groups.

Pet Profile

There are many different breeds of hamster. In nature, wild hamsters live in the deserts and plains of Central Asia. They range from the common Syrian hamster to the mouse-like Chinese hamster. Only certain breeds are kept as pets. Read more about their features to determine which type of hamster is best suited to your home.

Roborovski's

- Are golden-orange in color with a white belly
- Have white fur over their eyes, giving the appearance of white "eyebrows"
- Are the smallest type of pet dwarf hamster
- Have a calm personality
- Are lively and quick

Djungarians

- Are also called the Campbell's Russian hamster
- Have a fine black line from tail to ears
- Are dwarf hamsters
- Have a plump, round body shape
- Enjoy living in pairs, as long as they are introduced early in life
- Have fuzzy fur
- Are very friendly animals
- Have furry feet

Syrians

- Have many different **coat** lengths, ranging from hairless to long-haired
- Are the most common pet hamster
- Prefer to live alone
- Have hairless feet
- Are fierce fighters
- Come in a wide variety of colors, including gold

Chinese

- Have long tails
- Are mouse-like in appearance
- Have a dark stripe down their backs
- Are grayish-brown in color
- Have black-tipped ears
- Are difficult to breed since the females are extremely aggressive
- Have slender bodies

Siberians

- Are also called winter white Russians
- Have dark markings on their ears, nose, and tail
- Are gray and white in color
- Have fur that turns white in the winter
- Are originally from southwest Siberia
- Have a black stripe down their backs
- Get along well with other hamsters
- Are dwarf hamsters

Picking Your Pet

If you are thinking of getting a pet hamster, there are many factors you must consider. Make sure that no one in your family is allergic to pets before you bring home a hamster.

Which Type of Hamster Should I Get?

The most widely available breed of hamster is the Syrian hamster. Because they are larger than other breeds, Syrian hamsters are easier to handle. Other options include the Chinese hamster or Dwarf hamster. These breeds get along well together and can be kept in the same cage. However, they are much smaller than a Syrian hamster. This makes them difficult to handle, since they move very quickly.

Hamsters are solitary animals. This means that they usually live alone.

How Should I Prepare for My New Hamster?

Before you get a hamster, it is important to make sure that your home is safe for your new pet. If you have other family pets, you must be careful. Hamsters are unable to defend themselves against larger animals such as cats or dogs.

How Do I Pick a Healthy Hamster?

When you choose a hamster, check to see if he is healthy. You should examine his nose, mouth, ears, and bottom to ensure they are clean. His eyes should also be clear. A healthy hamster will have a shiny coat.

Hamsters are nocturnal animals. This means that they are active at night and sleep during the day. It is best to visit the pet store or breeder in the evening so that you can choose your hamster while he is awake.

Hamsters are omnivores. They enjoy eating both vegetables and meat.

Wild hamsters can store up to **60 pounds** of grain in their burrows. (27 kilograms)

Roborovski's hamsters are the shortest in length, at 1.5 to 2 inches. (3.8 to 5 cm)

The largest hamsters measure up to 13.5 inches in length. (34 cm)

The lightest hamsters weigh only about **1 ounce**. (20 grams)

Some hamsters weigh as much as **18 ounces**. (500 g)

Life Cycle

Your pet hamster's needs will vary, depending on her age. As she goes through each stage of development, she will require different kinds of care. Hamsters of all ages need plenty of love.

Newborn Hamsters

When hamsters are born, they are called puppies. Newborn puppies are very tiny, and almost completely helpless. They are deaf, blind, and furless. Although a newborn hamster cannot move very well, she is able to pull herself along using only her front feet. It is important to watch newborn hamsters and their mother very closely. Shy or young mother hamsters have been known to eat their puppies if they sense danger.

Two to Three Weeks Old

Between two and three weeks of age, hamsters have grown a soft, furry coat. They are alert and better able to move around. Hamsters at this stage are no longer solely dependent on their mothers' milk. They are just beginning to eat solid food and learning how to **hoard** it. At this age, hamsters may be a little wobbly. Sometimes, they may lose their balance.

Mature Hamsters

A hamster is considered full-grown when she is between five and six months old. At this age, she is now active, curious, and independent. An adult hamster requires many toys to keep her busy in her cage. Senior hamsters may need extra vitamins to stay healthy.

Five Weeks Old

At five weeks old, hamsters are ready to live on their own. They should not stay with their mother and littermates or else they may begin to fight. At this age, female hamsters are ready to have puppies of their own.

Gearing Up

There are many supplies required to properly care for your pet hamster. Before bringing him home, make sure that you have everything prepared. The most important piece of equipment you will need is a cage. It must be secure so that your hamster cannot escape. The best kind of cage is made of wire, with a plastic bottom. This will provide great climbing bars for your hamster. It will also ensure proper **ventilation**.

Toys, such as tunnels or tubes, can be a useful addition to your hamster's cage. They help keep your hamster physically and mentally active.

Buy a heavy food dish, water bottle, and plenty of nesting materials to put in your hamster's cage. It is important to line the floor with wood shavings. Do not use sawdust or cedar wood shavings, since these can be harmful to your hamster's health. Spread the wood shavings thickly along the bottom of the cage so that he can burrow in them.

Your hamster will need toys as well, such as climbing trees or gnawing logs. You can buy these from a pet store or use items from around your home. An empty toilet paper roll can be used as a tunnel. Hamsters are very active and love to play. An exercise wheel will keep your hamster healthy and happy. Be sure to find one with evenly spaced bars. If they are too far apart, his paws may get stuck.

Your hamster should also have a small house to sleep in. Never use cotton wool for your hamster's bed. He could eat it and become very ill.

Hamsters have **four clawed toes** on their front paws.

A hamster's back feet each have five toes.

Hamsters have a total of **16 teeth**.

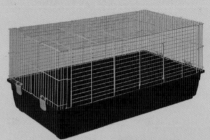

Your hamster's cage should be at least **15 inches** long and **12 inches** high. (38 cm long and 30 cm high)

Chinese hamsters are about 4 to 5 inches in length. (10 to 13 cm)

You should provide at least **2 square inches** of floor area per hamster. (13 square cm)

It is important to feed your hamster correctly. If she is overfed, she could become overweight.

Feeding Your Hamster

Your pet hamster should be fed in the early evening. This is when she is the most active. Unlike some pets, hamsters only require feeding once a day. It may look as if your hamster is still hungry once her food dish is empty. However, she has likely hidden food around her cage to eat later. Hamsters are known for being hoarders. She will find the food she has hidden later, when she is hungry.

If you feed your hamster fresh food, it is important to remove any leftovers in the morning. Otherwise, this food may spoil, which can make your hamster sick. Foods that are harmful to hamsters include chocolate, tomatoes, iceberg lettuce, and raw beans.

Make sure that your hamster always has a supply of fresh water to drink. Without water, she will become ill. A good option is a water bottle with a dispenser. This will keep the water clean, and prevent it from spilling in your hamster's cage.

Wild hamsters eat a variety of foods. These include roots, grains, insects, and anything else they are able to find. Your hamster will also need a variety of different foods to stay healthy. You can buy commercial hamster foods for your pet that help keep her diet well-balanced.

Hamsters love to eat snacks such as seeds, nuts, or dried vegetables. It is healthy to give your hamster treats a couple of times a week.

Built For Burrows

Although each breed of hamster has unique characteristics, all hamsters have certain features in common. Ranging from the tiny Roborovski's hamster to the large Syrian hamster, each breed has traits similar to the rest of the species. Hamsters all over the world are designed for life underground.

Scent Glands

A hamster's scent **glands** are found on his hips. He uses the musky liquid they produce to mark his territory and identify himself to other hamsters.

Paws

Hamsters use their paws for many things, including grooming, digging, holding food, and emptying their cheek pouches.

Eyes

Hamsters have large, bulging eyes. However, they do not see very well in daylight or at close range.

Ears

Hamsters have very good hearing. With their thin, delicate ears, they can hear sounds that people cannot.

Nose

Hamsters use their noses to identify food and other hamsters. They have a very good sense of smell.

Whiskers

Hamsters use their whiskers to help feel their way around. They act as sensors, and can detect nearby objects.

Cheeks

A hamster's cheek pouches can stretch all the way to his shoulder. They are used to store food.

Mouth

Hamsters have long upper and lower **incisors** at the front of their mouths. Their teeth never stop growing.

Hamster Housecleaning

Hamsters are naturally clean animals. They enjoy having their homes tidy and well-organized. You can also help keep your hamster's cage in good condition. It is important to clean out the cage on a regular basis. The tidier your hamster's cage, the more likely she is to live a long and happy life.

When cleaning out the cage, first empty its contents. Use hot, soapy water to scrub it clean. You can also use a spray to **disinfect** the cage. Be careful not to use a disinfectant with a strong scent. Hamsters are very sensitive, so ask your **veterinarian** for something mild but effective.

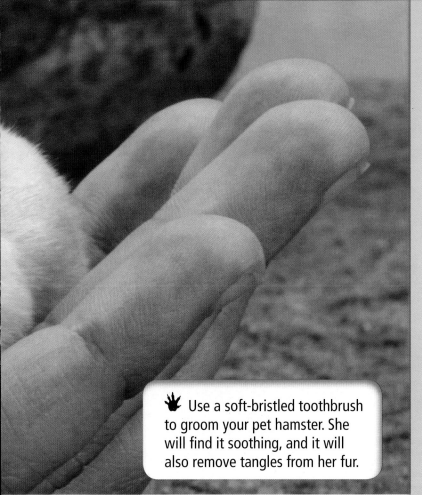

If your hamster has long hair, groom it _every day_.

If your hamster has short hair, groom it **once each week**.

Clean your hamster's litter **once a day.**

Change your hamster's bedding **once every week**.

Wash your hamster's cage **once a month.**

Use a soft-bristled toothbrush to groom your pet hamster. She will find it soothing, and it will also remove tangles from her fur.

Pay attention to the different areas of your hamster's cage. Hamsters will usually choose separate spots for sleeping, storing food, and going to the bathroom. It is important to keep each of these areas clean.

Make sure to keep your hamster's food dish and water bottle clean as well. You should check them on a daily basis. Save some of the bedding, wood shavings, and hoarded food to put back inside the cage when you are done. These familiar items will help your hamster feel comfortable in her newly cleaned home.

🐾 Hamsters enjoy running on wheels. Not only is it entertaining, this is also good exercise.

Healthy and Happy

In general, hamsters are healthy animals. If properly cared for, your pet hamster should not get sick often. Feeding him a balanced diet and cleaning his cage regularly will help ensure he stays healthy. The best way to keep your hamster active is with an exercise wheel.

There are other things you can do to prevent your hamster from becoming ill. Choosing the correct placement of his cage is especially important. It should be kept in a quiet area of your home. Hamsters can get stressed out if they are exposed to many loud noises. This can make them sick.

Make sure that you observe your hamster's behavior and habits. If you know how your hamster acts when he is well, you are more likely to notice if something is wrong. Watch for symptoms including a loss of appetite, dull coat, sneezing, inactivity, a wet tail, and a runny nose or eyes. These are all potential signs of illness. If you recognize any of these symptoms in your hamster, you should take him to the veterinarian right away.

The most common pet hamsters are Syrians, who live about **2 to 2 ½ years.**

Hamsters can run as much as **8 miles** each day. (13 kilometers)

The average litter size is between **four and eight** pups.

One human year is equal to about **25 hamster years**.

Hamster pups are born about **10 to 30 minutes** apart.

Handling Your Hamster

You must be very patient when getting a new hamster as a pet. Although you may want to play with her right away, it is important to wait until your hamster is ready to be handled. Hamsters may become scared if they are handled too soon. This can cause them to bite, out of fear. It is best to let your hamster settle in to her new home before you handle her.

Some breeds of hamster are more responsive to handling than others. Breeds that enjoy being held make friendlier pets.

The best way to make your hamster comfortable around you is to start by feeding her from your hand. Let her sniff your fingers, so that she comes to recognize your scent. Over time, she will feel safe enough for you to pick her up.

First, place one hand gently around your hamster's back. Wrap your fingers around her body and cup your other hand underneath her in a scooping motion. Eventually, your hamster will become comfortable with being held by you. She will even start to walk across your hands. Always make sure to hold your hamster close to the ground. This way, she will not get hurt if she falls or is accidentally dropped.

Hamsters can hold **0.63 ounces** of food in their cheek pouches. (18 g)

Give your pet hamster one to two days to adjust to her new surroundings.

Hold your hamster with two hands, or one hand held against your body.

When your hamster is ready, you can begin teaching her tricks. Try dangling a treat of food over her head. She will learn to stand on her haunches to reach it. Playing with your hamster can be a rewarding experience for both pet and owner.

Pet Peeves
Hamsters do not like:

To add variety to your hamster's diet, give her fresh fruit such as grapes, apples, or bananas, as a treat.

- being squeezed or held too tightly, especially if their cheek pouches are full
- being played with or handled during the daytime
- being startled while sleeping
- eating sticky or sharp foods that may get stuck in their cheek pouches

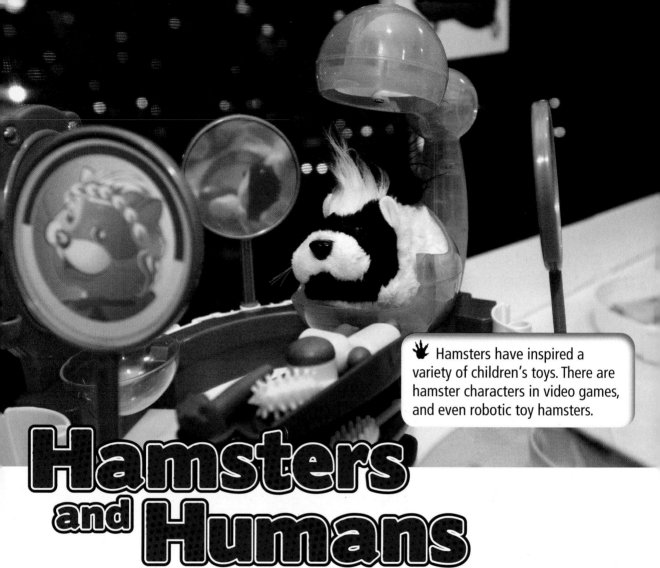

Hamsters have inspired a variety of children's toys. There are hamster characters in video games, and even robotic toy hamsters.

Hamsters and Humans

Throughout the years that people have kept hamsters as pets, these tiny creatures have brought much joy and amusement to their owners. Hamster owners are often extremely proud of their furry companions. Some even enter their pet hamsters into competitions.

During a professional hamster show, the animals are judged and given prizes for their features, such as the quality of their coat. There are hamster associations that offer information about the different hamster breed standards. These help determine whether or not your pet hamster can be shown at a competition.

Hamsters can be found in popular culture as well. They have been featured in many stories, movies, and television shows. They are often depicted as mischievous and energetic. In *Hamsters Don't Glow in the Dark*, Abby's pet hamster escapes and goes on an adventure.

Perhaps the most famous hamster in popular culture is Hammy the Hamster. He lives in an old boot on a beautiful riverbank where he has many fun experiences with his friends. Hammy the Hamster teaches audiences how to appreciate the natural environment. Every show includes a lesson about the importance of being respectful of all animals.

Most hamsters are descendants of three litter mates domesticated in 1930.

Some hamsters can blink **one eye** at a time.

In the wild, hamsters can dig tunnels up to **33 feet** in length. (10 meters)

🐾 Popular television show *The Simpsons* features a recurring hamster character named Nibbles.

Pet Puzzlers

What do you know about hamsters? If you can answer the following questions correctly, you may be ready to own a hamster.

1. What is the best way to make your hamster comfortable around you?

Start feeding her from your hand, so she can pick up your scent

2. How much should you feed your hamster each day?

0.2 to 0.4 ounces of dry food (5 to 10 g)

3. When do hamsters grow their fur?

Between two and three weeks of age

4. What does the term "nocturnal" mean?

Active at night and asleep during the day

5. What are some signs your hamster may be ill?

Loss of appetite, dull coat, sneezing, inactivity, a wet tail, and runny nose or eyes

6. How many teeth does a hamster have?

16

7. Which is the smallest breed of pet dwarf hamster?

Roborovski's hamster

8. What are a hamster's cheek pouches used for?

Storing food

9. Where was the first hamster discovered?

In the deserts of Syria, near Aleppo

10. How many breeds of hamster are kept as pets?

Five

Holler for your Hamster

Before you buy your pet hamster, brainstorm some hamster names you like. Some names may work better for a female hamster. Others may suit a male hamster. Here are just a few suggestions.

Fluffy

Teddy

Cheeky

Buster

Snowflake

Sandy

Ginger

Hammy

Patches

Key Words

burrowed: dug a hole or tunnel deep in the ground

coat: an animal's fur

disinfect: kill harmful germs using chemicals

extinct: no longer in existence

glands: special organs that produce scents

hoard: save for future use

incisors: teeth used for cutting or gnawing

rodents: mammals with teeth designed for nibbling or gnawing

ventilation: constant fresh air

veterinarian: animal doctor

zoologist: a scientist who studies animals

Index

Log on to www.av2books.com

AV² by Weigl brings you media enhanced books that support active learning. Go to www.av2books.com, and enter the special code found on page 2 of this book. You will gain access to enriched and enhanced content that supplements and complements this book. Content includes video, audio, weblinks, quizzes, a slide show, and activities.

AV² Online Navigation

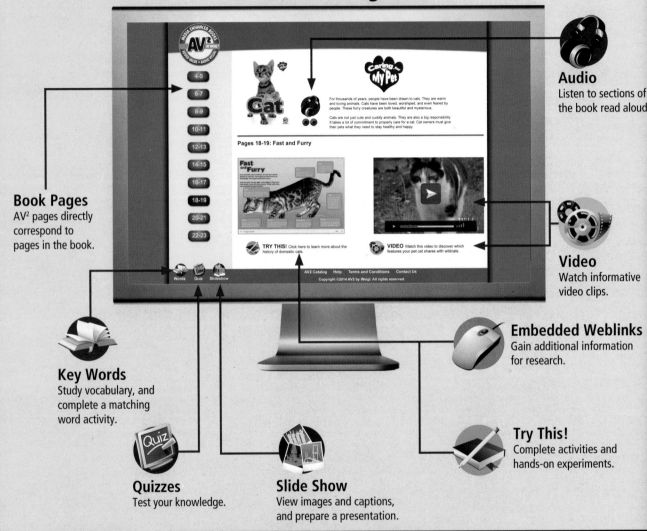

Book Pages
AV² pages directly correspond to pages in the book.

Audio
Listen to sections of the book read aloud

Video
Watch informative video clips.

Key Words
Study vocabulary, and complete a matching word activity.

Embedded Weblinks
Gain additional information for research.

Quizzes
Test your knowledge.

Slide Show
View images and captions, and prepare a presentation.

Try This!
Complete activities and hands-on experiments.

AV² was built to bridge the gap between print and digital. We encourage you to tell us what you like and what you want to see in the future.

Sign up to be an AV² Ambassador at www.av2books.com/ambassador.

Due to the dynamic nature of the Internet, some of the URLs and activities provided as part of AV² by Weigl may have changed or ceased to exist. AV² by Weigl accepts no responsibility for any such changes. All media enhanced books are regularly monitored to update addresses and sites in a timely manner. Contact AV² by Weigl at 1-866-649-3445 or av2books@weigl.com with any questions, comments, or feedback.